POCKET BOOK OF
FRIENDSHIP

First published in Great Britain 2020 by Trigger

Trigger is a trading style of Shaw Callaghan Ltd & Shaw Callaghan 23 USA, INC.

The Foundation Centre

Navigation House, 48 Millgate, Newark

Nottinghamshire NG24 4TS UK

www.triggerpublishing.com

British Library Cataloguing-in-Publication data

A CIP catalogue record for this book is available upon request
from the British Library

ISBN: 9781789561845

Trigger Publishing has asserted their right under the Copyright,
Design and Patents Act 1988 to be identified as the author of this work

Cover design and typeset by Fusion Graphic Design Ltd

Printed and bound in China by Hung Hing Printing Group Ltd

Paper from responsible sources

POCKET BOOK OF

FRIENDSHIP

TRIGGER™
The mental health & wellbeing publisher

www.triggerpublishing.com

the *Shaw* mind
FOUNDATION

INTRODUCTION

Modern life can be filled with so much: from the daily commute, a hectic schedule, cooking an evening meal; to those crucial turning points: quitting your job, moving house, finding love. Between the noise, it can be hard to make and maintain friendships.

The *Pocket Book of Friendship* offers a little guidance for when the scales of life are tipped, times are turbulent and a moment of companionship is needed. From the minds of some of the world's most well-known figures, learn to prioritise your friendships and truly value your loved ones, even when times are tough.

Be true to your work, your word,
and your friend

Henry David Thoreau

Friends show their love in times of trouble,
not in happiness

Euripides

My books are friends that never fail me

Thomas Carlyle

Share your smile with the world.
It's a symbol of friendship and peace

Christie Brinkley

We come from homes far from perfect,
so you end up almost parent and
sibling to your friends – your own chosen
family. There's nothing like a really loyal
dependable, good friend. Nothing

Jennifer Aniston

Be a friend to thyself,
and others will be so too

Thomas Fuller

I don't like that man.
I must get to know him better

Abraham Lincoln

A friend is someone who knows
all about you and still loves you

Elbert Hubbard

Friends are the best to turn to
when you're having a rough day

Justin Bieber

Seek not the favor of the multitude;
it is seldom got by honest and lawful means.
But seek the testimony of few;
and number not voices, but weigh them

Immanuel Kant

I have learned that to be with
those I like is enough

Walt Whitman

There are no strangers here;
only friends you haven't yet met

William Butler Yeats

I cannot even imagine where I would be today were it not for that handful of friends who have given me a heart full of joy

Charles R. Swindoll

Age appears best in four things:
old wood to burn, old wine to drink,
old friends to trust and old authors to read

Sir Francis Bacon

Friendship is the wine of life

Edward Young

He who sows courtesy reaps friendship,
and he who plants kindness gathers love

Saint Basil

The language of friendship is
not words but meanings

Henry David Thoreau

The best way to mend a broken heart
is time and girlfriends

Gwyneth Paltrow

Friendship consists in forgetting what one gives and remembering what one receives

Alexander Dumas

There is nothing on this earth more to be
prized than true friendship

Thomas Aquinas

I never considered a difference of
opinion in politics, in religion, in philosophy,
as cause for withdrawing from a friend

Thomas Jefferson

One of the most beautiful qualities
of true friendship is to understand
and to be understood

Seneca

My two best girlfriends are from secondary school. I don't have to explain anything to them. I don't have to apologize for anything. They know

Emma Watson

There is no enjoying the possession
of anything valuable unless one has
someone to share it with

Seneca

If we treated ourselves as
well as we treated our best friend,
can you imagine?

Meghan Markle, Duchess of Sussex

"Stay" is a charming word in
a friend's vocabulary

Louisa May Alcott

My definition of a friend is somebody
who adores you even though they know
the things you're most ashamed of

Jodie Foster

Man's best support is a very dear friend

Cicero

Friendship at first sight,
like love at first sight,
is said to be the only truth

Herman Melville

Friendship is the only cement
that will ever hold the world together

Woodrow Wilson

True friends are like diamonds — bright, beautiful, valuable and always in style

Nicole Richie

A man's friendships are one of the
best measures of his worth

Charles Darwin

Friendship is like money,
easier made than kept

Samuel Butler

Friendship is not always the
sequel of obligation

Samuel Johnson

Friendship is the hardest thing in the world to explain. It's not something you learn in school. But if you haven't learned the meaning of friendship, you really haven't learned anything

Muhammad Ali

There is no friendship that cares
about an overheard secret

Alexandre Dumas

Love is the only force capable of
transforming an enemy into a friend

Martin Luther King, Jr.

Rare as is true love,
true friendship is rarer

Jean de La Fontaine

The process of falling in love at first
sight is as final as it is swift in such a case,
but the growth of true friendship
may be a lifelong affair

Sarah Orne Jewett

The shifts of fortune test
the reliability of friends

Cicero

I don't know what I would have done so many times in my life if I hadn't had my girlfriends

Reese Witherspoon

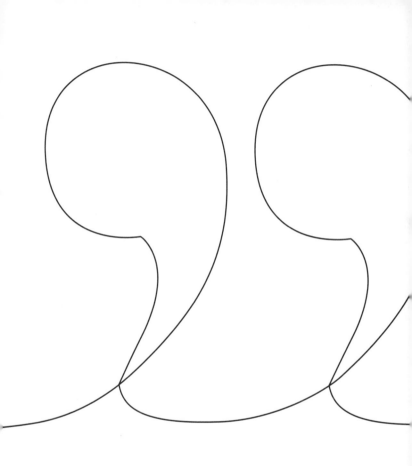

Of all the means to ensure happiness
throughout the whole life,
by far the most important is the
acquisition of friends

Epicurus

There can be no friendship
without confidence, and no confidence
without integrity

Samuel Johnson

A true friend unbosoms freely, advises justly,
assists readily, adventures boldly, takes all
patiently, defends courageously,
and continues a friend unchangeably

William Penn

True friendship is a plant of slow growth,
and must undergo and withstand the
shocks of adversity, before it is entitled
to the appellation

George Washington

It is not a lack of love,
but a lack of friendship that
makes unhappy marriages

Friedrich Nietzsche

There is nothing more admirable than
when two people who see eye to eye
keep house as man and wife,
confounding their enemies and
delighting their friends

Homer

Be slow in choosing a friend,
slower in changing

Benjamin Franklin

Lots of people want to ride with
you in the limo, but what you want is
someone who will take the bus with
you when the limo breaks down

Oprah Winfrey

One loyal friend is worth ten
thousand relatives

Euripides

Friendship is the source of the greatest pleasures, and without friends even the most agreeable pursuits become tedious

Thomas Aquinas

Women's friendships are
like a renewable source of power

Jane Fonda

There is nothing I would not do for those who are really my friends. I have no notion of loving people by halves, it is not my nature

Jane Austen

To throw away an honest friend is,
as it were, to throw your life away

Sophocles

I really believe you are the company
you keep and you have to surround yourself
with people who lift you up because
the world knocks you down

Maria Shriver

False friendship, like the ivy, decays and ruins the walls it embraces; but true friendship gives new life and animation to the object it supports

Richard Burton

If you have one true friend you
have more than your share

Thomas Fuller

There is no happiness like that of being
loved by your fellow creatures,
and feeling that your presence is an
addition to their comfort

Charlotte Brontë

Friendship improves happiness and
abates misery, by the doubling of our joy
and the dividing of our grief

Cicero

A friend is a gift
you give yourself

Robert Louis Stevenson

As iron sharpens iron,
so a friend sharpens a friend

King Solomon

A friend to all is a friend to none

Aristotle

Experts on romance say for a happy
marriage there has to be more than a
passionate love. For a lasting union,
they insist, there must be a genuine
liking for each other ...

... which, in my book, is a good definition for friendship

Marilyn Monroe

Find a group of people who challenge
and inspire you; spend a lot of time with
them, and it will change your life

Amy Poehler

Sweet is the memory of distant friends

Washington Irving

Friendship is one mind in two bodies

Mencius

The best part about having true friends is
that you can go months without seeing them
and they'll still be there for you ...

... and act as if you'd never left

Ariana Grande

Love is flower-like;
Friendship is a sheltering tree

Samuel Taylor Coleridge

I know, firsthand, that soccer
brings people together – all it takes is
a ball and a few people, and the seeds
of friendship are planted

Ali Krieger

I was tired of pretending
that I was someone else
just to get along with people ...

... just for the sake of having friendships

Kurt Cobain

Be courteous to all, but intimate
with few, and let those few be well tried
before you give them your confidence

George Washington

The best thing to hold
onto in life is each other

Arthur Schopenhauer

It is more shameful to
distrust our friends than to be
deceived by them

Confucius

Do I not destroy my enemies
when I make them my friends

Abraham Lincoln

Truth springs from
argument amongst friends

David Hume

"

The ideal friendship is to
feel as one while remaining two

Sophie Swetchine

It's the friends you can
call up at 4 a.m. that matter

Marlene Dietrich

It is easier to forgive an enemy
than to forgive a friend

William Blake

Friendship is essentially a partnership

Aristotle

There are no rules for friendship.
It must be left to itself

William Hazlitt

No one is useless in this world
who lightens the burdens of another

Charles Dickens

My friends are my estate

Emily Dickinson

Friendships are discovered rather than made

Harriet Beecher Stowe

Perhaps the most delightful
friendships are those in which there
is much agreement, much disputation,
and yet more personal liking

George Eliot

The world is so empty if one thinks
only of mountains, rivers and cities;
but to know someone who thinks
and feels with us ...

... this makes the earth for us
an inhabited garden

Goethe

I love my husband, but it is nothing like
a conversation with a woman
that understands you. I grow so much
from those conversations

Beyoncé

He will never have true friends who is
afraid of making enemies

William Hazlitt

Friends are proved by adversity

Cicero

Look, whatever happens,
I'll always be there for you and
you're never in this life on
your own against the world ...

... you've always got a mate
looking out for you

Declan Donnelly

66

A quarrel between friends, when made up,
adds a new tie to friendship

Saint Francis de Sales

Friendship increases in visiting friends,
but in visiting them seldom

Sir Francis Bacon

The feeling of friendship is like that of
being comfortably filled with roast beef;
love, like being enlivened with champagne

Samuel Johnson

We hate some persons because we do not know them; and will not know them because we hate them

Charles Caleb Colton

Of all the things that are beyond my power,
I value nothing more highly than to
be allowed the honor of entering into
bonds of friendship with people
who sincerely love truth

Baruch Spinoza

The better part of one's life
consists of his friendships

Abraham Lincoln

Words are easy, like the wind;
Faithful friends are hard to find

William Shakespeare

The best friend is the man who in
wishing me well wishes it for my sake

Aristotle

The worst part of success
is trying to find someone
who is happy for you

Bette Midler

Friendship is the finest balm
for the pangs of despised love

Jane Austen

All love that has not friendship for its base,
is like a mansion built upon the sand

Ella Wheeler Wilcox

Marriage is the highest state of friendship.
If happy, it lessens our cares by dividing
them, at the same time that it doubles our
pleasures by mutual participation

Samuel Richardson

Friendship may, and often does, grow into love, but love never subsides into friendship

Lord Byron

There is no friendship, no love,
like that of the mother for the child

Henry Ward Beecher

The best mirror is an old friend

George Herbert

You find out who your real
friends are when you're
involved in a scandal

Elizabeth Taylor

What do we live for,
if it is not to make life less
difficult for each other

George Eliot

The best time to make friends
is before you need them

Ethel Barrymore

At the shrine of friendship never say die,
let the wine of friendship never run dry

Victor Hugo

Associate yourself with people of
good quality, for it is better to be alone
than in bad company

Booker T. Washington

We must reach out our hand in friendship
and dignity both to those who would befriend
us and those who would be our enemy

Arthur Ashe

True friendship ought never
to conceal what it thinks

Saint Jerome

True friendship comes when the silence
between two people is comfortable

David Tyson

No matter how tired I am,
I get dinner at least once a week
with my girlfriends. Or have a sleepover.
Otherwise my life is just all work

Jennifer Lawrence

What's helped me is having really good friends I know I can rely on

Drew Barrymore

A friend is a beloved mystery;
dearest always because he is not ourself,
and has something in him which it is
impossible for us to fathom. If it were not so,
friendship would lose its chief zest

Lucy Larcom

Without friends, no one would want to live,
even if he had all other goods

Aristotle

For a little guidance elsewhere ...

POCKET BOOK OF

HAPPINESS

For when life gets a little tough

POCKET BOOK OF

HOPE

For when life gets a little tough

The mental health & wellbeing publisher

www.triggerpublishing.com

We want to help you to not just survive
but thrive ... one book at a time

Find out more about Trigger Publishing by visiting our website:
triggerpublishing.com or join us on:

@TriggerPub

A proportion of profits from the sale of all Trigger
books go to their sister charity, The Shaw Mind Foundation,
founded by Adam Shaw and Lauren Callaghan.

The charity aims to ensure that everyone has access
to mental health resources whenever they need them.

Find out more: **shawmindfoundation.org** or join them on:

@Shaw_Mind   @ShawMindFoundation   @Shaw_Mind